Mental Toughness For Teens

Harness The Power Of Your Mindset and Step Into A More Mentally Tough, Confident Version Of Yourself!

Jennifer Williams

© **Copyright 2022 - All rights reserved.**

The content contained within this book may not be reproduced, duplicated or transmitted without direct written permission from the author or the publisher.

Under no circumstances will any blame or legal responsibility be held against the publisher, or author, for any damages, reparation, or monetary loss due to the information contained within this book, either directly or indirectly.

Legal Notice:

This book is copyright protected. It is only for personal use. You cannot amend, distribute, sell, use, quote or paraphrase any part, or the content within this book, without the consent of the author or publisher.

Disclaimer Notice:

Please note the information contained within this document is for educational and entertainment purposes only. All effort has been executed to present accurate, up to date, reliable, complete information. No warranties of any kind are declared or implied. Readers acknowledge that the author is not engaged in the rendering of legal, financial, medical or professional advice. The content within this book has been derived from various sources. Please consult a licensed professional before attempting any techniques outlined in this book.

By reading this document, the reader agrees that under no circumstances is the author responsible for any losses, direct or indirect, that are incurred as a result of the use of the information contained within this document, including, but not limited to, errors, omissions, or inaccuracies.

Table of Contents

Introduction **8**

How to Use This Book..9

Chapter 1: Understanding How Your Mind Views Fear And Anxiety **12**

Brain Vs. Mind: The Ground-Breaking Difference Not Many People Know 12

Transforming your Unconscious Mind....................................... 14

Hack Your Thoughts to Shape a Future That Excites You 16

Discover Your Deep-Rooted Fears and Treat Your Subconscious Mind..17

Chapter 2: Conquer Your Mindset And Put An End To The Negative Loop **26**

Your Personal Secret Weapon: Thinking................................... 26

How to Become Proactive and Stay One Step Ahead Of Your Own Mind... 29

How Cognitive Distortions Are Undermining Your Success 30

Chapter 3: Challenging your Negative Thinking and Gaining Confidence in your Judgment **39**

Challenging Your Negative Thinking... 39

Chapter 4: How Mental Toughness Can Help You Stand Out In School **47**

Shaping a Positive Mindset Towards School and Education 47

How to Break Free from a Fixed Mindset and Enter a Growth Mindset 49

Chapter 5: Overcoming Rejection And Coming To Terms With Your Emotions **55**

Rejection = Redirection 55

How to Learn from Failure and Get Back on Your Feet 57

Chapter 6: Rejecting The Need To Give Up 61

Don't Give Up 61

Controlling Your Behaviors 65

Chapter 7: BONUS CHAPTER: Standing Your Ground When Dealing With Difficult People 68

How to Connect with Difficult People 68

Developing Empathy and Understanding 69

Setting your Boundaries Clearly and Effectively 72

Saying No to Unacceptable Actions and Behavior 73

Conclusion 79

References 81

Your Free Gifts !

Out of all of the available literature on this subject, you chose this one. Thank you. As a way to express my gratitude, I'm offering additional valuable resources for FREE to my readers.

10 video Presentations, 10 Workbooks, 10 eBooks, 10 Cheetsheets, 10 Audio Files, 10 Checklists, 10 Mindmaps.

Unlock proven strategies for coping with Trauma, Resentment, Failure, Disappointment, Feeling out of Control, Lack of Meaning, Existential Crisis, Loss of Grounding, Major Changes, and Overwhelming times with **FREE** access to my 10 eCourses.

Each course includes a video presentation, workbook, eBook, cheatsheet, checklist, Audio file, and Mindmap, valued at over $9,000.

Get access to proven strategies and tools to improve your inner peace and well-being today!

Get Free Instant Access by clicking on or going to

learnfromjenwilliams.com/Jen-Free-Gifts

eCourse #1 - 10 Successful Coping Strategies For Dealing With **Trauma And Traumatic Events.** Includes Video Presentation, 35-page Workbook, eBook, Cheetsheet, Checklist, Audio file & Mindmap! *Minimum Value: $1,897.* **You get it FREE!**

eCourse #2 - 10 Successful Coping Strategies For Dealing With **Major Changes When Life Is Turned Upside Down.** Includes Video Presentation, 77-page Workbook, eBook, Cheetsheet, Checklist, Audio file & Mindmap! *Minimum Value: $699.* **You get it FREE!**

Your Free Gifts !

eCourse #3 - 10 Successful Coping Strategies For When **Resentments Are Ruining Your Inner Peace.** Includes Video Presentation, 62-page Workbook, eBook, Cheetsheet, Checklist, Audio file & Mindmap! *Minimum Value: $836.* You get it FREE!

eCourse #4 - 10 Successful Coping Strategies When You Feel Your **Life Is Out Of Control.** Includes Video Presentation, 46-page Workbook, eBook, Cheetsheet, Checklist, Audio file & Mindmap! *Minimum Value: $679.* You get it FREE!

eCourse #5 - 10 Successful Coping Strategies For When You Feel Your **Life Has No Meaning Or Purpose.** Includes Video Presentation, 71-page Workbook, eBook, Cheetsheet, Checklist, Audio file & Mindmap! *Minimum Value: $592.* You get it FREE!

eCourse #6 - 10 Successful Coping Strategies For When You Are **Reeling From Failure.** Includes Video Presentation, 64-page Workbook, eBook, Cheetsheet, Checklist, Audio file & Mindmap! *Minimum Value: $992.* You get it FREE!

eCourse #7 - 10 Successful Coping Strategies For When You Are Going Through An **Existential Crisis.** Includes Video Presentation, 80-page Workbook, eBook, Cheetsheet, Checklist, Audio file & Mindmap! *Minimum Value: $571.* You get it FREE!

eCourse #8 - 10 Successful Coping Strategies For When You Have **Lost Your Centre And Don't Feel Grounded.** Includes Video Presentation, eBook, Cheetsheet, Checklist, Audio file & Mindmap! *Minimum Value: $392.* You get it FREE!

eCourse #9 - 10 Successful Coping Strategies For Dealing With Major **Disappointments In Your Life.** Includes Video Presentation, 88-page Workbook, eBook, Cheetsheet, Checklist, Audio file & Mindmap! *Minimum Value: $1,043.* You get it FREE!

eCourse #10 - 10 Successful Coping Strategies For Overwhelm And **Overwhelming Times**. Includes Video Presentation, 43-page Workbook, eBook, Cheetsheet, Checklist, Audio file & Mindmap! *Minimum Value: $1,362.* You get it FREE!

Before we start, I have a small favor to ask of you. When you finish reading this book, **would you please consider posting a review of this book on the platform?** Posting a review is incredibly valuable for a small independent author like me and will help support my writing. Thank you. I really appreciate it.

Just use the relevant link below.

USA - https://amazon.com/review/create-review/?&asin=B0BTJ4JB8W

UK - https://amazon.co.uk/review/create-review/?&asin=B0BTJ4JB8W

Canada - https://amazon.ca/review/create-review/?&asin=B0BTJ4JB8W

Introduction

Don't wait until everything is just right. It will never be perfect. There will always be challenges, obstacles, and less than perfect conditions. So what? Get started now. With each step you take, you will grow stronger and stronger, more and more skilled, more and more self-confident, and more and more successful.

- Mark Victor Hansen

Are you tired of feeling mentally weak and lacking confidence? Do you want to harness the power of your mindset and become a more mentally tough and confident person?

Look no further!

This book provides practical tips and strategies to help you unlock your full potential and achieve your goals. From learning how to manage negative thoughts to setting achievable goals, you'll discover how to cultivate a positive mindset and become the strongest version of yourself. I've cut through the fluff and only brought you the essentials. I have removed the irrelevant information and provided you with a concise and effective solution.

You'll learn how to overcome your negative thinking, and cultivate a confident and resilient outlook on life. Whether you're an athlete, a student, or just someone looking to improve their mental toughness, this book is for you.

I will cover a variety of techniques, strategies, and exercises to help you develop a growth mindset, increase self-awareness, and boost self-esteem. By following the tips and strategies outlined here, you'll discover a newfound sense of mental toughness and confidence. You'll be better equipped to tackle obstacles and reach your goals, no matter what life throws your way.

The power of mindset is undeniable when it comes to personal growth and success. We've all heard the saying, "Mind over matter," and it couldn't be more true. Our thoughts and beliefs have a profound impact on our lives, and a positive, and mentally tough mindset can help us overcome obstacles, achieve our goals, and lead a fulfilling life.

In the bonus chapter at the end of this book, I will show you practical and effective techniques to handle conflicts, communicate effectively, and maintain a positive attitude even in the face of adversity. No more feeling frustrated and stressed. You will develop a confident and empowered approach to dealing with difficult people.

A mentally tough mindset can help you overcome obstacles, achieve your goals and create a fulfilling life. In this book, you will learn how to harness the power of your mindset and become a less anxious and more confident version of yourself in sport, school and life!

How to Use This Book

There are times when I look at my two teenage children and silently say a prayer for them. The truth of the matter is that we are living in the most challenging times in history, where violence, perversion, and peer pressure are just some of the challenges our children are faced with.

This isn't to say that back when I was a teenager, these social ills didn't exist. However, we grew up in a time when society was still relatively conservative and governed by traditional values. For example, even though I suffered from self-esteem issues that were due to peer pressure, it wasn't blown out of proportion by social media. I didn't have access to toxic online content designed to make me doubt myself.

Therefore, even though a part of me can relate to the challenges faced by my two modern teens, another part can only imagine the amount of stress, anxiety, and temptations they contend with on a daily basis.

As a mother, teacher and coach for children in sports, I am passionate about the empowerment of young people. I know it sounds cliché, but I do believe that young people represent the future of our country and the world at large. I feel personally responsible to ensure that the upcoming generations are equipped to confront and overcome the mental, emotional, and physical challenges of this modern age. This is what made me compile this book and do my part to ensure that modern teens know what it means to be mentally tough.

There are many different words for mental toughness, such as resilience, mental discipline, champion attitude, or growth mindset. All of these words describe the ability to get up from every setback and continue moving forward.

Mental toughness is the insurance that helps you survive hardships. It doesn't take away your problems, but he can make your problems seem less overpowering. In other words, you regain a sense of control in your life and see yourself as being an overcomer -

somebody who cannot be shaken or discouraged by the highs and lows of life.

The value found inside this book is hidden in the practical exercises and step-by-step techniques that you will be taught. Without committing yourself to practicing these exercises, it will be difficult to cultivate mental toughness. Success in anything in life requires hard work and the same applies to learning life skills like resilience and self-discipline. What you learn from this book can change your life, but only if you take action.

The secret of transformation is to apply the information, rather than just reading over it. If you are ready to learn what it means to be mentally tough and rise above the modern challenges of this age, continue reading!

Chapter 1: Understanding How Your Mind Views Fear And Anxiety

As you sow in your subconscious mind so shall you reap in your body and environment.

- Joseph Murphy

In this chapter you will learn:

- The difference between the conscious and subconscious mind.
- The importance of healthy subconscious programming.
- Four therapeutic techniques to explore your subconscious mind.

Brain Vs. Mind: The Ground-Breaking Difference Not Many People Know

The terms brain and mind are often used to refer to the same thing - the three-pound mass of grey matter in between your ears. But the truth is they refer to two different, but related entities.

You have probably learned about the brain in biology. The simplest way to define the brain would be an organ covered by your skull that helps you breathe, walk, talk, and think. We call the experts at focus primarily on researching the brain, neuroscientists. Through their studies and reports, neuroscientists are able to tell us which bodily functions or human reactions are affected by different regions of the brain.

For instance, they can detect, through brain scans, when the brain is not receiving, processing, recording patterns, or storing information properly. And since the brain and body are linked through nerves, neuroscientists can also trace poor brain health to poor diet, high blood pressure, lack of quality sleep, or not getting enough physical exercise. Taking care of your brain boils down to making certain healthy lifestyle changes and reducing the amount of stress you are exposed to.

If all of the information I have shared so far refers to your brain, what exactly is the mind? Well, the mind is not a physical organ that you can see or touch. It is your human psyche and takes the information processed by the brain and interprets it as thoughts, feelings, memories, beliefs, and behaviors. You can think of the mind as the non-physical part of your brain that creates human experiences and gives your life a sense of meaning.

The brain has no conception of right or wrong, good or evil. It cannot help you make the right choices or change your perspective on certain situations. On an evolutionary level, the brain is quite basic in function. Apart from receiving, processing, recording patterns, and storing information, its powers are limited. However, when used in conjunction with the mind, the information that is received through your senses can become thoughts and feelings.

The reason why it is important for you to know that your brain and mind are two separate entities is that it can improve the way you manage tasks and emotions. For example, when you sense a feeling of frustration, you will understand that it is an experience produced by the mind, based on information that has been processed, recorded, are stored by the brain. In other words, a feeling is not just a feeling that comes out of nowhere. It can be traced back to the information received from your environment.

Transforming your Unconscious Mind

So far, you know where your thoughts come from. But it's time to go a little deeper and explore how thinking occurs in the mind. The terms "conscious" and "subconscious" are used in the field of psychology to describe mental states. Each mental state serves its unique purpose, and none is greater than the other. The main difference between the two mental states is the basic human functions each controls and how they guide cognitive processes.

The conscious mind is the part of the mind that is aware of what is taking place in the here and now. It allows you to think on your feet, make decisions, brainstorm ideas, and solve immediate problems. Paying attention, logical reasoning, and rationalizing processes are all functions of the conscious mind.

Since this part of the mind is aware of what is happening in the present moment, it is in charge of interpreting the cues, pictures, words, and activities that come from your environment through your five senses and sending messages to your subconscious mind.

The subconscious mind is the part of your mind that is unconscious, or "asleep." Its job isn't to manage day-to-day tasks and decision-making like your conscious mind, but instead to interpret the information that you receive on a daily basis. Depending on your programs that the subconscious mind uses to interpret information, such as your past memories, habits, beliefs, and values, or unresolved traumas, the type of feedback it will communicate back to the conscious mind will be positive or negative.

A simple analogy to explain this phenomenon is the backend of a website. Think of the subconscious mind as the code that powers the website (conscious mind). The visitors who come to the website cannot see the long code, but they can see the graphics, banners, and other cool website features that the code created. The same applies to your subconscious mind. Even though you are not aware of your subconscious mind (and the beliefs, habits, memories, or traumas that help to interpret information), the state of your subconscious mind can still be seen in your actions and responses to everyday life situations.

The relationship between the conscious and subconscious mind usually creates a dilemma: sometimes, the information that is received through the five senses isn't interpreted for what it is – it is interpreted through subconscious programming. It is, therefore, not uncommon to find that your reactions to certain life situations don't match what is taking place in reality.

For example, if the sound of a dog barking makes you feel anxious, it may have more to do with your subconscious programming than the actual barking. After all, a dog barking only seems dangerous if you have a negative memory of being attacked by a dog. Someone who doesn't have that kind of negative association with a dog's bark probably won't respond in fear when hearing that sound.

Subconscious programming can also affect how you perceive yourself, your beliefs about life, and how to relate to other people.

When your programming is healthy (meaning that your habits, beliefs, memories, and values are healthy), you can develop a positive self-esteem and be more open to taking risks and developing healthy relationships with others.

However, when your programming is unhealthy, your perception of yourself and reality becomes clouded with negative beliefs and habits that make life feel threatening and cause you to think poorly of yourself and others. To gain control of your mind, you must first evaluate the kind of subconscious programming you are operating under. This is usually where personal transformation begins - at a subconscious level. Once you have reprogrammed your subconscious mind, your actions and responses to life will naturally change and reflect the quality of your improved programming.

Hack Your Thoughts to Shape a Future That Excites You

I'm sure you have probably heard of cyber criminals known as hackers. They are genius coders who use their incredible computer programming skills to break into computer systems, so they can steal, destroy, or manipulate information. Once they hack into a system, they are able to access confidential data that individuals and companies wouldn't want anyone to know about.

Hacking is also the term used in the field of psychology to refer to accessing the subconscious mind. If you think about it, the only way to access this unconscious part of the mind is to bypass the conscious mind and travel along mental pathways that no one has travelled before.

Throughout this book, I will show you various strategies to hack your subconscious mind in order to adjust your thinking and development mental toughness. The reason why we will be working mainly on the subconscious level is that this is where true transformation begins. If you want to think differently, you must start by changing your thinking patterns, and this can only be done by hacking your subconscious mind.

Many people wouldn't think to solve mental and emotional problems on a subconscious level. They think to themselves, "why hack your subconscious mind when you can read an empowering book, get a lecture from your parents, or listen to a podcast? But the truth is that unless you change or adjust your subconscious programming, the same negative thoughts, feelings, and behaviors that disappear while reading a good book will reappear and you put the book down.

Discover Your Deep-Rooted Fears and Treat Your Subconscious Mind

Before we get deep into the strategies, I must add a disclaimer. The process of hacking the subconscious mind isn't as glamorous as it may sound. As soon as you start going deeper and deeper into your mind, you are likely to remember past painful memories, fears from childhood, secrets that you had forgotten, and any other upsetting thought or emotion that you had bottled up many years ago.

As you dig up these programs, who might start to feel tearful, angry, confused, or uncomfortable. It is also common to enter a reflective state of mind, where you think about the timeline of your life and the various moments that have made your life meaningful.

To keep your mind open, calm, and balanced as you go deeper into your subconscious mind, you can practice specific therapeutic techniques that are designed to help reflect, increase awareness, and express what is coming up in your mind. They can also help you understand and regulate intense emotions that arise during the process. Below are four therapeutic techniques that will continuously be brought up as you read this book.

1. Deep Breathing Techniques for Anxiety

Deep breathing, also known as diaphragmatic breathing, is a technique that reduces stress and anxiety, lowers blood pressure, and induces a feeling of relaxation. When you are overwhelmed with emotion, it is normal for your heart rate to accelerate and your blood pressure to shoot up, which can make you feel anxious. You may also notice your breathing pattern changing; taking shorter, irregular breaths rather than slow and deep breaths.

The purpose of deep breathing is to deliberately slow down your breathing so that your body can return to its normal, restful state. A basic deep breathing exercise that you can practice whenever you want to feel calm is box breathing.

]The instructions go as follows:

- Sit on a chair or stand upright.
- Slowly exhale out of your mouth, getting as much air out of your lungs.

- Create a mental picture of a box in your head, with four equal sides.

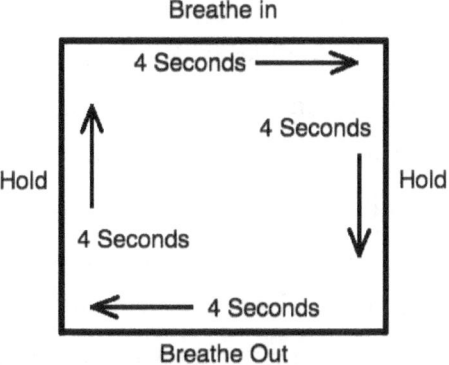

- Inhale through your nose and count up to four slowly. As you count, imagine that you are working your way along the top of the box (moving horizontally).
- Hold your breath for another four counts. Mentally picture yourself making your way down the box (moving downward).
- Slowly release the breath out of your mouth for another four counts, this time working your way along the bottom of the box (moving horizontally).
- Finally, hold your breath for four counts and imagine that you are making your way up the side of the box to complete the full box. (moving upward).
- Repeat the pattern two or three times.

2. Meditation to Help you Grow and Gain Clarity

One of the best ways to increase self-awareness and tap into your subconscious mind is to practice meditation. Originally, meditation was used as a spiritual exercise in Eastern traditions to increase consciousness. Over the centuries, it has been adapted to Western traditions and used as a psychological tool to reduce stress and anxiety, improve concentration, and increase awareness of your thoughts and feelings. The meditative act of tuning into your inner world is what allows you to observe your mind and notice thoughts, beliefs, emotions, and memories that are floating around.

Below is a basic meditation script that you can practice to become more familiar with the structure. Record yourself reciting the script in a slow and gentle voice, then isolate yourself in a quiet room and play the recording.

- Sit down in a comfortable position, either on the floor or on a chair.

- Make sure that your spine is lengthened, shoulders dropped, and arms hanging loosely beside you.

- Close your eyes and begin to breathe normally. Focus on your breathing until there are no longer any mental distractions.

- When you are ready, begin the box breathing exercise. Imagine that your breath follows the perimeter of a box. Inhale for four counts, hold your breath for four counts, exhale for another four counts, and complete the box by holding your breath for four counts.

- Notice the rhythm of your breathing. Is it consistent or irregular? Now consider the pace of your breathing. Would you say it is slow or fast?

- Notice any physical sensations that are flowing through your body. Where are these sensations coming from? How subtle or intense are they?

- If there is any discomfort or tension in your body, focus your breath on that area. As you exhale, mentally picture your breath moving to that area and bringing instant relief. Repeat this as many times as you need to.

- Finally, accept positive intentions and release negative thoughts and feelings through your breath.

- Inhale and picture yourself breathing in a positive emotion or desire, like peace or loving relationships. Allow the breath to travel all the way to your belly and hold it for a few seconds.

- As you exhale, imagine that you are pushing out all of the fear, anxiety, or stress that has been circulating throughout your body. Feel the force of negativity make its way up from your lungs and out through your mouth. Repeat this as many times as you need to.

- Prepare to end the meditation by breathing normally again. Wiggle your toes and stretch your fingers to regain feeling in your body. Open your eyes and sit in silent contemplation for a few more seconds before getting up.

3. Positive Affirmations

Positive affirmations are intentional statements that are interpreted as commands by your subconscious mind. Over time, these statements are able to adjust your subconscious programming and change how you think and view yourself and others. The trick to creating powerful affirmations is to speak in definitive terms, such as using "I am" statements, because this causes your mind to believe that what you are declaring is already taking place at this very moment.

To get yourself in the habit of reciting positive affirmations, set out 15 minutes, either in the mornings or evenings, to go through your list. You can either record your affirmations and play the recording, repeating after yourself, or you can look into a mirror and declare your affirmations out loud. The best kinds of positive affirmations are those that you come up with on your own. However, below is a list of affirmations to get you inspired.

- I am confident in who I am.
- I set the pace in my life.
- I take pride in my solitude.
- Every mistake is a learning opportunity in disguise.
- I am an asset.
- I am allowed to ask for help.
- I deserve to live a good life.
- I am doing the best that I can.
- I am growing stronger and wiser each day.

- I am in control of my thoughts and emotions.
- I am worthy of being loved.
- I am optimistic about today.
- I am a magnet for opportunities.
- I am supported by a loving community.
- I am passionate about my life.

4. How to Start Journaling Your Thoughts

Do you remember the stage where everybody had a diary, and they would spill all of the juicy stories about their friendships and romantic lives? Nowadays, diaries are not used for sharing gossip, but more as a tool to vent frustration, describe complicated feelings, or reflect on beliefs and past childhood memories.

Just the simple act of writing is therapeutic enough. Once that pen hits the paper and you completely allow yourself to be open and share what you are thinking and feeling, you can relieve stress and anxiety. Plus, being vulnerable with your life experiences makes it possible to gain deeper insight into hidden desires, emotional wounds, fears, and beliefs. Over time, reading over what you have written will enable you to identify patterns from the past, and how they might show up in the present moment.

Some people prefer to journal about the first topic or thought that comes to their mind, while others would rather use journal prompts for more guided responses. Below are some journal prompts that you can use to get started with your journaling practice.

- When you look at yourself in the mirror, what do you see?
- What is your favorite childhood memory?
- If you would go back in time, what year would you go back to, and why?
- How would you describe yourself?
- What motivates you to wake up every morning?
- Who are the people who matter most to you, and why?
- If money was not a factor, what type of lifestyle would you live?
- What values do you consider most important in your life?
- Finish the sentence: When I am feeling discouraged, I pick myself up by...
- Finish the sentence: The place where I feel safest is...

Chapter Takeaways

- The brain and mind are often seen as being the same thing, but they are not. The brain is responsible for receiving, recording, and storing information, while the mind interprets and extracts meaning from it.

- How your mind interprets information determines how you think, what you believe, and how you behave. Negative actions and poor decision-making are the results of harmful subconscious programming that distorts information being fed to your mind.

- The only solution for improving your mindset and upgrading your thinking patterns is to hack your subconscious mind and change or adjust the programs. Throughout this book, you will be taught various ways of doing this, so don't worry—you are in safe hands!

In the next chapter, you will learn more about negative thinking patterns; how they are formed, and the various ways they can influence your beliefs, attitudes, and behaviors.

Chapter 2: Conquer Your Mindset And Put An End To The Negative Loop

Fear starts in the mind and it generates emotions. One fearful thought will lead to another if you let it.

–Sadie Robertson

In this chapter you will learn:

- The different types of thinking patterns, and what happens when you entertain negative thoughts.
- How to identify and break the cycle of negative thinking.

Your Personal Secret Weapon: Thinking

Thoughts are mental representations of the outside world. Depending on what your subconscious mind is trying to make sense of, thoughts can take the shape of ideas, opinions, or beliefs.

By nature, thoughts are subjective because they are created from your perspective. However, depending on how you look at a situation, your thoughts can be rational or irrational, fact or emotion-based.

The mind engages in different types of thinking, which are known as thinking patterns. These patterns can be simplistic, like perceptual thinking, or more complex, like critical thinking. To give you an understanding of the different ways you think, below is a list of five thinking patterns.

1. Perceptual Thinking

Perceptual thinking refers to perceiving reality based on your previous life experiences. For example, you might feel anxious before taking a science test because you think that you are going to fail. Unfortunately, this type of thinking does not allow you to see another person's point of view because it is solely based on your perceptions.

2. Abstract Thinking

Compared to perceptual thinking, this is a more broad and flexible type of thinking. It involves exploring different ideas and concepts about life, going beyond your mental boundaries, and seeking higher knowledge. When you embrace abstract concepts, you are consciously going outside of your comfort zone and learning about different perspectives that might challenge your own understanding of life.

3. Reflective Thinking

One of the most utilized types of thinking during the process of changing subconscious programming is reflective thinking. This is because reflective thinking focuses on understanding past experiences recorded in the mind. It seeks to break down past events, assess the emotional impact, weigh the pros and cons, and create a sense of meaning so that you can have a better understanding of yourself and others.

4. Creative Thinking

Albert Einstein famously said, "Insanity is doing the same thing over and over and expecting different results". In order to solve complex problems, Einstein knew that creativity—and a hint of imagination—was necessary. Creative thinking, similar to abstract thinking, is about questioning how things are and exploring new ways of solving old problems.

5. Critical Thinking

The opposite of perceptual thinking is critical thinking. It involves setting aside your opinions and beliefs and sorting through facts to solve problems. The type of skills that are required to think critically are the ability to process, analyze, and draw patterns from information to arrive at an unbiased conclusion.

For instance, going back to the example about feeling anxious for a science test, thinking critically would require you to find factual evidence of previously failing a science test to validate your limiting belief. If no evidence of failing a test can be found, then that belief would be seen as faulty.

As you can tell, the type of thinking pattern you utilize determines how you interpret the world around you. Sometimes, you might interpret life events from your own limited perspective, which may or may not block you from seeing the bigger picture. Other times, you might interpret life events with wisdom gained from reflecting on past life experiences.

The point that I am trying to make is that how you think of things matters, and it is important to become more aware of the thinking patterns you are engaging in at any particular moment.

How to Become Proactive and Stay One Step Ahead Of Your Own Mind

Now that you know the different ways you can think, we can go a little deeper and explore how thinking patterns can be corrupted with negative thoughts. However, before going further, it is important to emphasize that negative thoughts are natural.

When you are overcome with unpleasant emotions, like anger, fear, suspicion, or doubt, it is common to make unrealistic assumptions, become judgmental of yourself and others, or even adopt a warped perception of reality. In most cases, all it takes to adjust negative thoughts is to remind yourself that not everything you think is necessarily true and that sometimes emotions can feel like facts—even though they are not.

Negative thoughts only become an issue when they control your thinking patterns and cause you to perceive your life, relationships, and capabilities from a negative perspective. When this occurs, you are more likely to develop cycles of negative thinking, also called cognitive distortions.

A typical cycle often goes like this: A negative thought becomes a negative belief, which leads to negative coping strategies and behaviors that ultimately reinforce the negative thought. For as long as negative thoughts are left unchallenged, the cycle continues.

Over time, your thinking patterns become so corrupt that all information received through your senses is interpreted through negative subconscious programming. You can go as far as perceiving healthy relationships as dangerous or feeling like you are unlovable and deeply flawed.

The good news is that you can identify cycles of negative thinking by learning how to recognize cognitive distortions. When this happens, it becomes a lot easier to challenge your negative thoughts!

How Cognitive Distortions Are Undermining Your Success

Cognitive distortions are simply errors in the way you think. They cause you to look at the world in a distorted, unrealistic, or imbalanced way. Instead of accepting reality for what it is, they cause you to jump to conclusions, or come up with the worst-case scenarios in your head.

It is also important to note that cognitive distortions can create false beliefs that end up distorting how you look at yourself, others, or the world. For example, believing that you are undesirable just because your relationship status is "single" can lead to self-esteem issues. Therefore, whenever cognitive distortions are identified, they must be replaced with more realistic and balanced thoughts that can support your growth.

Below are just a few examples of cognitive distortions, as well as how they might sound in your mind.

1. All-Or-Nothing Thinking

All-or-nothing thinking, also known as black-or-white thinking, occurs when you view a situation as being extremely good or extremely bad, with no middle ground. You might use polar opposite terms to describe people or situations, like good or evil, friend or enemy, and love or hate. This type of thinking leaves no room for compromises because circumstances are seen in a fixed way.

Example: "I need to get an 'A' for my test. A 'B' average is just not good enough."

Can you think of a few more examples of all-or-nothing thinking? Write them down on the line space provided below.

_____

_____

_____

_____

_____

_____

2. Emotional Reasoning

Emotional reasoning refers to making conclusions based on how something feels, rather than on the objective truth about the situation. It is usually difficult to spot when you are using emotional reasoning because emotions can sometimes feel like facts. For example, if you dislike someone, you can easily misjudge them and paint them as a bad person. Nonetheless, emotions are not reliable because they are subjective and cannot give you the full picture of what is taking place in any given situation.

Example: "I feel anxious about making new friends, therefore making new friends must be dangerous."

Can you think of a few more examples of emotional reasoning? Write them down on the line spaces provided below.

_____

_____

_____

_____

_____

3. Overgeneralization

Overgeneralization occurs when you place too much significance on a past experience (most cases being a negative experience) and use it as a deciding factor on how to act in the present moment. The main belief is that what happened once is likely to happen again. However, this is not always true. Old patterns, beliefs, and experiences are only brought forward into your current life if you decide to hold onto them.

Example: "I was terrible at sports when I was in primary school. There is no point in me trying out for sports in high school."

Can you think of a few more examples of overgeneralization? Write them down on the line space provided below.

_____

_____

_____

4. Labeling

Labeling is a natural mental process of assigning names and categories to people, places, and situations. The brain does this to create mental shortcuts so that you do not have to remember how you feel or respond to certain things. The issue with labeling, however, is that it makes it difficult to accept reality for what it is or engage with people for who they truly are. When you are fixated on labels, your experience of life is limited, which makes it that much harder to embrace change.

Example: "I am stupid and won't get very far in life."

Can you think of a few more examples of labeling? Write them down on the line space provided below.

_____

_____

_____

_____

_____

_____

5. Jumping to Conclusions

You may have spoken casually to a friend and told them to "Stop jumping to conclusions" whenever they were trying to guess what you were going to say without getting all of the facts. Jumping to conclusions is another type of cognitive distortion that occurs whenever a negative assumption is made in the absence of information. Unless you are able to find evidence that proves this assumption to be untrue, you may be convinced that it is actually valid.

Example: "My parents create house rules as a way to punish me."

Can you think of a few more examples of jumping to conclusions? Write them down on the line space provided below.

_____
_____
_____
_____
_____

6. Mental Filtering

Mental filtering refers to considering the negative side of a situation and overlooking the positive. In real-life, this might be seen in how you can easily remember the negative memories about your childhood but can't seem to remember many positive memories. Over time, mental filtering can lead to the belief that your life is only full of negative experiences and very few positive experiences.

Example: Believing that as a child you were always alone, even though you had a loving and supportive family by your side.

Can you think of a few more examples of mental filtering? Write them down on the line space provided below.

7. Mind Reading

Mind reading is similar to jumping to conclusions. You assume that you know a person's intentions or how a situation will end up. It is impossible to know what someone else is thinking or feeling without asking them directly. In relationships, mind reading can lead to misunderstandings and hurt feelings because you or the other person aren't given a chance to express your genuine thoughts and feelings.

Example: My friend is taking longer to respond to my text. She must be upset with me.

Can you think of a few more examples of mind reading? Write them down on the line space provided below.

8. Catastrophizing

Have you ever felt worried about a situation and made it bigger than it actually was? If so, you were caught up in a cognitive distortion known as catastrophizing. When this occurs, a minor situation is magnified, and you tend to think of the worst-case scenarios. In other words, you make a mountain out of a molehill.

Example: "Being rejected by that hot girl has ruined my chances of ever falling in love."

Can you think of a few more examples of catastrophizing? Write them down on the line space provided below.

_____

_____

_____

_____

_____

_____

9. The Inability to Be Wrong

It is impossible to know everything because you can only see the world through your perspective, and don't have an infinite amount of the skills, knowledge, and life experience. Therefore, at times, it is normal to be in the wrong. Thinking that you are always right, even when you are inexperienced in a particular subject is a sign of a cognitive distortion. The more balanced way of looking at life is assuming that there is something you can learn from everyone you meet.

Example: "I know what I'm talking about. My opinions are stronger than yours."

Can you think of a few more examples of the inability to be wrong? Write them down on the line space provided below.

_____

_____

_____

_____

_____

_____

10. Personalization

Personalization occurs when you take information or circumstances that have nothing to do with you and find a way to make them personal. For example, you might assume that a friend's silence is due to something you did wrong, or that your girlfriend canceled a date because they don't want to spend time with you.

Example: "My mother is stressed because of having to take care of me."

Can you think of a few more examples of personalization? Write them down on the line space provided below.

_____

_____

_____

___

___

___

Please note that not every negative thought will fit under the distortions mentioned above. Some negative thoughts may even fall under more than one category. The aim is to be aware of the different ways that your thoughts can be misleading so that you don't blindly accept them as being true.

Chapter Takeaway

- It is possible to escape the negative thought loop. All you need to do is pause and evaluate your thoughts before acting upon them.

Chapter 3: Challenging your Negative Thinking and Gaining Confidence in your Judgment

Positive thinkers think and talk continually about solutions, and negative thinkers continually talk and think about problems. Keep your mind solution-focused rather than problem-focused.

–Brian Tracy

In this chapter you will learn:

- Cognitive techniques to challenge negative thoughts and positively reframe your mind.

Challenging Your Negative Thinking

Once you are aware of negative thoughts, it becomes a lot easier to challenge and replace them with more balanced beliefs and perspectives. Cognitive techniques are useful skills that teach you how to adjust your thinking and see your life circumstances from a wider perspective. Grab a pen and go through each of the cognitive techniques mentioned below!

Reframing Cognitive Distortions

When you are faced with a challenging situation, your mind will try to make sense of what is happening around you. In order to do this, it has to produce a thought. In most cases, thoughts produced during stressful times are distorted due to the limited information you have to look at the situation objectively.

Getting into the habit of challenging your thoughts can help you identify cognitive distortions before they become fixed beliefs. The exercise below will help you identify different types of cognitive distortions and replace them with balanced thoughts.

Look at the table below and write down the appropriate cognitive distortion that is associated with each thought. Thereafter, provide an alternative thought that is less distorted and more grounded in facts.

Original thought	Type of cognitive distortion (Negative Thinking)	Alternative thought
"If I don't attend the party, my friends will never speak to me again."		
"I know exactly what I'm talking about. I don't need to listen to you."		

"Either I'm picked to play for the league, or I will sit out of the game."		
"I feel left out because nobody is talking to me."		
"It is my fault that my parents don't speak to each other."		
"I got heartbroken when I opened up to someone. I don't think it is safe to open up again."		
"I'm the dumbest kid in the class."		
"My life has always been chaotic. Things never work out for me."		

"If she really cared about me, she would have asked if I was okay."		

Recharging your Thoughts with Emotions

Strong emotions can, at times, trigger certain thoughts that reinforce how you are feeling. Whenever you notice a change in your mood, notice the changes in your thought patterns as well. Record the changes in your thoughts inside a journal, so you can keep track of your thought patterns.

Look at the tables below and familiarize yourself with the different thoughts that are triggered by strong emotions. Feel free to add your own thoughts where it says "Other."

When I am feeling **DEPRESSED**, I think...
I am a failure.
Everyone thinks I am dumb.
I don't deserve true friendships.
There is no point in being social if no one likes me.

Other:

When I am feeling **ANXIOUS**, I think...
Something bad is going to happen.
I can't cope with this.
I need to get away from everyone.
What are people thinking about me?
Other:

When I am feeling **ANGRY**, I think...
No one understands me.
I need to defend myself.
I can't get over this.

| I hate everybody. |
| Other: |

Regaining Control Over Your Mental Blocks

Cognitive distortions can sometimes create mental blocks; these are limiting beliefs that prevent you from maximizing your full potential and living a fulfilling life. Mental blocks usually start with "I can't" or "I don't" and create self-imposed limits. One of the best ways to overcome mental blocks is to provide evidence that proves you are capable and can successfully achieve your desires. Note that this evidence must be based on facts and grounded in reality. For example, you can mention a past accomplishment that proves you are capable of achieving a current goal.

Complete the table below by providing evidence to disprove the mental block.

Mental block	**Positive evidence to disprove the mental block**
I don't have enough patience to read a whole book.	

I can't make friends because of how different my personality is.	
I don't think I have what it takes to lose weight.	
I just can't take it anymore.	
Nobody will ever understand me.	
I don't enjoy going out.	
I only won based on sheer luck.	
I'm not as good as everybody thinks.	
I'm too busy.	
I can't bring myself to concentrate.	

Chapter Takeaways

- Remember, not every thought is reliable, especially those that provoke you to react in negative ways. It is up to you to police your thoughts and replace those that won't produce the kind of positive life outcomes you desire.

So far, we have explored how the brain and mind function, as well as how thoughts lead to actions and behaviors. Below are a few lines that you can use to reflect on what you have learned so far. When you are ready, we will take an in-depth look at what being "mentally tough" entails, and various strategies to cultivate mental toughness.

_____

_____

_____

_____

_____

_____

_____

_____

_____

_____

_____

_____

Chapter 4: How Mental Toughness Can Help You Stand Out In School

Do the best you can until you know better. Then when you know better, do better.

–Maya Angelou

In this chapter you will learn:

- How your mindset shapes your attitudes and behaviors about school.

- The difference between a fixed and growth mindset, and practical ways to adopt a growth mindset when faced with school challenges.

Shaping a Positive Mindset Towards School and Education

Not every teenager's experience of school is the same. There are those who have a positive attitude toward school, those who dread the idea of a formal education, those who beat themselves down for not achieving academic success, as well as those who may enjoy some aspects of school, like being able to play sports and socialize, but are not interested in the rest.

You fit somewhere in between these categories of students and may have your own personal views about school. However, beyond liking or disliking school, one thing is for sure: Your goal is to make it through high school as painlessly as possible! To achieve this goal, your mindset about school matters.

Author and psychologist, Carol S. Dweck, found that a student's mindset about school originated from the quality of thoughts they held about it. For example, students who had a negative perception of school tended to fear challenges or were afraid to make mistakes. On the other hand, students who held flexible thoughts about school showed more openness to embracing challenges, could easily bounce back from setbacks, and appreciated the process of learning.

Dr. Dweck summarized these two types of mindsets as representing fixed and growth mindsets (Dweck, 2006). Students with a fixed mindset are those who may not believe they can work on their weaknesses and improve their school performance over time. They see themselves as being stuck at the current level they were at and feel hopeless about their educational progress. These students are more likely to entertain thoughts such as:

- "I will never be an A student."
- "Math is just not for me."
- "I always mess up."
- "There is no point in trying."
- "I'm not as smart as the other kids."

In contrast, students with a growth mindset believe that their skills can improve over time. They see the process of learning as being continuous, meaning that after achieving one educational goal, they can go on to achieve another one. Making mistakes isn't something they fear because those mistakes can be corrected and new lessons learned, thus even failure has the potential to be a teachable moment. Some of the thoughts that these students are more likely to entertain include:

- "I may not be an A student now, but with time and dedication, I have the potential to be!"
- "I need more support with Math."
- "I learn from my mistakes."
- "I learn something new every time I try."
- "Nobody is born smart. With time, I can become the kind of student I admire."

Dr. Dweck concluded that students obtaining a growth mindset were more likely to improve in school performance, owing to the amount of hard work they were willing to put in, and their high level of resilience.

How to Break Free from a Fixed Mindset and Enter a Growth Mindset

Since the brain is malleable, it is possible to adjust your mindset and go from rigid to flexible thinking. All it takes to slowly adopt a growth mindset concerning school is to be open to learning different ways of thinking about school.

Say to yourself, "I may feel this way about school, but this is not the full picture." You must be willing to stretch your mind and start to see things differently. Below are three strategies that will kickstart your journey from a fixed to a growth mindset:

1. Make Different Choices

If you are used to responding to school stress or approaching school tasks in a negative way, such as leaving homework for the last minute or failing to meet deadlines, make different choices. Start working on your homework as soon as you get it, and shock yourself by submitting it early (if possible).

You can also get in front of bad communication habits by learning to reach out for help when you need it, whether it is from your friends, parents, or teachers. If you have a particular sport goal, you can make a choice to dedicate more time to training or studying the theory behind the sport, so you can improve your performance.

2. Set Academic Goals

Academics may or may not be your strong point, but that doesn't mean you cannot improve in that area of your school life. As part of making different choices, set goals for each test or subject. Besides academic goals, you can look at other areas of your life that would benefit from improvements, such as your social life. An example of a social goal that you can set would be making a new friend or deepening your relationships with existing friends.

3. Make a Fuss About Your Achievements

Celebrating your big and small achievements gives you a reason to continue persevering. Don't downplay any kind of "win," even if it may not be a big deal to your peers. For example, if it is your first time answering all of the questions on a test before running out of time, that is an achievement worth celebrating! Your brain will appreciate the rush of dopamine and will reward you by feeling proud of yourself. Other examples of small wins include initiating conversations with new people, completing household chores without being reminded, or handing in your assignments on time. These may not be considered goals worth celebrating for most people, but they mean something to you!

Above and beyond these three strategies, the questions below will help you understand the difference between a fixed and growth mindset, and practical ways you can adopt a growth mindset to your learning.

1. When you consider setting goals for your grades, what is the first thought that comes to mind? Would that be an example of a fixed or growth mindset? E.g., I tend to think "I don't know if I can do that." This is an example of a fixed mindset.

2. When you are faced with challenges at school, like not doing well on a test, how do you typically respond? Would your response be an example of a fixed or growth mindset? E.g., I tend to look back at previous tests where I performed well and encourage myself that one bad mark won't jeopardize my entire grade. This is an example of a growth mindset.

3. When a teacher gives you feedback on your performance, how do you take it? Would your reaction be an example of a fixed or growth mindset? E.g., When I receive feedback, I feel personally attacked. I feel the need to defend myself, rather than listen and apply the feedback. This is an example of a fixed mindset."

4. When your school friends succeed, such as receiving recognition for achieving outstanding results, how does that make you feel? Would your response be an example of a fixed or growth mindset? E.g., I tend to celebrate with them because it inspires me to work hard. This is an example of a growth mindset.

5. Think of a particular subject you are struggling with. What is one common mistake you make when learning the subject that you can improve? E.g., When learning math, I tend to overlook the need to memorize my times tables. I can improve by allocating 10 minutes each day to studying multiples of one specific number.

_____
_____
_____
_____
_____

6. What are the different ways you can ask for help when you don't understand a concept or instruction? Write down the different phrases or strategies you can use. E.g., I can write down a list of questions on paper and present them to my teacher after class.

_____
_____
_____
_____
_____

7. How can you improve your time management as a student? Write down different strategies that fit your lifestyle. E.g., Dividing my homework time into 10-minute slots, with 2-minute breaks in between, so I can achieve intense focus without too many distractions.

Chapter Takeaways

- Every student has their own ideas and opinions about school, but what is common amongst students is their desire to complete high school as painlessly as possible. Changing your mindset can reduce the stress and anxiety you have about school and cause you to regain a sense of control and make better choices.

- When you have a fixed mindset, you may perceive school as being harder or more depressing than it is. The fixed mindset blocks you from having an open attitude toward challenges and believing that you can improve your performance.

- The best type of mindset to have about school, as Dr. Dweck suggests, is a growth mindset. This type of mindset encourages you to rise above setbacks and believe that with time, you can become the kind of student you desire to be!

Now that you know how to apply mental toughness at school, the following chapter will explore how mental toughness can be applied to overcoming rejection and failure.

Chapter 5: Overcoming Rejection And Coming To Terms With Your Emotions

Keep pressing forward in spite of rejection. It doesn't matter how many no's you get. You only need one person to say yes.

–Germany Kent

In this chapter you will learn:

- How two of the most successful people in the world turned their rejection into motivation to achieve their dreams.

- Five valuable life lessons that you can only learn by failing at something.

Rejection = Redirection

When you think about becoming successful, what kind of picture appears in your mind? Do you imagine living in a luxury house, located in a gated neighborhood, over the hills? Or opening your 10-car garage door and having the option of choosing which supercar you would like to take for a spin?

The kind of success that is glorified on social media shows only one side of success—in most cases, the side that gets you to dream about dropping out of school and starting your own multi-million-dollar tech business! However, this isn't all that success is about.

In fact, in order to become successful, you must first encounter a lot of failure and rejection. Yes, you read correctly! Contrary to what you may have read, success doesn't come from making the best decisions; it comes from making a lot of bad decisions and choosing to learn from them.

Think of J.K. Rowling, the author of the book series, *Harry Potter*, who was a single, unemployed mother of one who lived off welfare benefits to support herself and her child. During the time of writing the first Harry Potter manuscript, she was 20 years old and diagnosed with clinical depression. But fortunately, she had a talent for writing, which became her source of encouragement.

After completing the manuscript, Rowling approached several publishers to score herself a book deal. She was rejected by 12 publishing houses before she signed a deal with Bloomsbury. In total, she heard 12 "Nos" before receiving a multi-million pound "Yes."

Then there is Walt Disney, who not only influenced our childhoods with his enchanting fairy tales but also built what is popularly known as the "Happiest Place in the World," Disney World. When pitching the idea for the Disney World theme parks, bankers thought he was out of his mind!

He was turned down 300 times for loans at the bank and eventually decided to take out money from his own pocket, and borrow from friends and family, to get the project off the ground. Imagine what would have happened if he decided to give up after the 50th or 100th rejection. How different would the world of media, animation, and entertainment look today?

Successful people who manage to overcome rejection and pursue their goals regardless of the challenges they are faced with, understand that being rejected doesn't mean that it is the end of the road. It simply means that whatever strategy you were applying isn't working, and you should move on to the next one. For them, rejection is a form of redirection that gets them closer to achieving their dreams.

How to Learn from Failure and Get Back on Your Feet

When you hit rock bottom and come to the realization that what you had hoped to achieve may not actually happen, it can be a painful experience. There is nothing enjoyable about going from being in control and on top of your game one minute, then all of a sudden, losing all control and returning to ground zero.

However, this too is only one side of failure. There is another side of failure (just as there is another side of success) which can be encouraging. Nobody talks about this side of failure because it is positive—and let's face it, who wants to think positively when they are down in the dumps?

The truth is that failure can teach you more about life than your victories can. Instead of seeing it as a life event, you can choose to see failure as a tool that helps you avoid repeating certain mistakes again. Every time your plans fail, you gain valuable insight into what works and what doesn't. This allows you to go back to the drawing board, make a few tweaks, and execute the plan again. If you fail the second time, at least you won't be repeating the same mistakes; you will be making new mistakes and correcting them so that your next execution is better than the last one!

What does all of this mean? To put it simply, failure allows you to gain experience, and with experience comes wisdom. You are better off having failed a few times before achieving your goals than accomplishing your goals on the first try. This is because you learn so much about yourself and the desires you are chasing after, each time you redirect. There are a number of life lessons that only failure can teach you. Below are my top five:

1. Stay Humble

At times, when pursuing goals, you can feel invincible, as though no challenge is big enough to get in your way. But failure teaches you that in the grand scheme of life, what you know is very limited, and there are a whole bunch of factors that are out of your control. This lesson is humbling because it exposes your own weaknesses and allows you to approach life, and other people, with more patience, open-mindedness, and respect.

2. Create Your Own Opportunities

When Plan A fails, what do you do? Well, most people would simply give up. Very few people would realize that they have the power to create new opportunities. In most cases, failure reveals gaps in your planning. For example, you may have miscalculated how much it would cost to purchase a brand new lemonade stand.

Now you are left with two options: Abandon your lemonade business idea or find another cost-effective way to purchase (or build) a lemonade stand. To create your own opportunity, you might decide to have a look in your backyard for scrap pieces of wooden planks. A bit of DIY work, and before you know it, you have built a sturdy stand. How you perceive failure determines whether you are able to create an opportunity out of it.

3. Embrace Change

Failure teaches you that not everything will always work out exactly as you imagined it would. For example, along the journey of pursuing your goal, you may be forced to make compromises, like completing your physical workouts at home instead of the gym to save on costs. Or maybe you experience sudden life changes that force you to postpone your goals for a few months while sorting the issue out. Being open to change can help you remain focused on your goals but flexible enough to adjust how you achieve them.

4. Be Creative

When you decide to take the traditional route to achieve your goals and your plans don't end up going as they should, you get the chance to embark on an unconventional route, a path that you create for yourself. To succeed on the new path, you are encouraged to think out of the box and do things a little differently. For example, if studying using parrot learning doesn't help you achieve the results you are looking for, you might try studying with pictures or by listening to audio.

5. *Trust Yourself*

One of the best lessons you can learn from failure is to trust yourself. No matter how much time you spend strategizing, your plans can still fail. And no matter how much faith you place in people, they can still disappoint you. But whether your plans fail, or people disappoint you, you are always there to pick yourself up after a setback and try again. Failure teaches you to listen to your gut instinct, show self-compassion, and develop confidence in your own abilities. After every setback, you get up stronger and more fearless than you were before.

Chapter Takeaways

- Success has two sides: The glamorous lifestyle that money can afford you, as well as the many rejections you need to encounter on the journey to achieving your dreams. You cannot become successful without first experiencing the hardship that develops you into the kind of person who is fearless and resilient.

- Similar to success, failure also has two sides. On the one hand, failure can be humiliating and cause you to lose everything you have worked hard to achieve. But on the other hand, it can teach you valuable lessons about life, and expose you to the kinds of experiences that help you make better choices.

Chapter 6: Rejecting The Need To Give Up

It always seems impossible until it's done.

– Nelson Mandela

In this chapter you will learn:

- How to get rid of the "I quit" mentality and never entertain giving up again!

Don't Give Up

If being confronted with obstacles is a part of life, your best bet is learning how to protect yourself from the "I quit" mentality. When things are not looking up for you at school, home, or in your relationships, it is important to remind yourself that giving up is not an option, unless of course, you find yourself in toxic situations.

The "I quit" mentality tends to sound like this:

- "Nothing is working out."
- "Why is it taking so long?"
- "This is more difficult than I thought."
- "Nobody is supporting me."
- "I keep making the same mistakes."
- "What was I thinking to even start this?"

- "Maybe this isn't a good time to pursue my goal."

When you replay these thoughts, over and over in your head, you will eventually give yourself enough reasons to give up. Therefore, it is important to detect the "I quit" mentality during the early stages and counter-attack with positive beliefs that will convince your mind that you actually CAN achieve your goals. Below are five positive beliefs that you can recite in the mirror or whisper to yourself whenever you think about quitting.

1. Belief: I Keep Every Commitment I Make to Myself

Your word is your honor. Whenever you commit to doing something, it is your job to make sure that you don't disappoint yourself. Every time a promise is broken, you chip away at your ability to trust what you say. Therefore, even when you don't feel like it, show yourself that you can maintain your word.

At school: When you look at your study plan and feel overwhelmed by the amount of information you need to absorb, remind yourself that your brain has the capacity to learn.

In sports: When your fitness regimen looks difficult, remind yourself that no challenge is impossible to achieve when you are determined to conquer it.

2. Belief: I Will Either Find a Way or Create One

The challenges you face in life shouldn't distract you from your goal. Whether Plan A works or fails, your main focus should be achieving your goal. You can avoid the temptation to abandon your goal by reminding yourself that you have plenty of options on how to arrive at your desired outcome. If there isn't a clear path to getting there, convince yourself that you can create one!

At school: When you don't understand a concept taught, despite how many times it has been explained, look for different teaching methods online that can help you understand the concept better.

In sports: If there is a specific technique that you cannot master, despite how much you try, sit down with your coach and ask for more notes or practical tips to help you learn the technique.

3. Belief: I Have the Ability to Find a Solution

You are smarter than you think. Just look at all the uncomfortable situations you have been able to overcome in the past. When you feel as though you have reached a dead end, tell yourself that you have the ability to find a solution. There is no problem that is too complicated for you to figure out. And when you need a second opinion, you can always reach out to people who have experienced the same kinds of challenges you are facing right now.

At school: When you are experiencing difficulty in a particular subject, get a second opinion. Be willing to ask your teacher questions on how to solve different problems. If you cannot speak to your teacher, find a classmate who understands the subject better and pose your questions to them.

In sports: If you would like to get better at playing a sport, read books or watch videos related to the sport to expand your knowledge. You can also follow popular sports players you admire and study their techniques.

4. Belief: Setbacks Are Temporary

Failure is inevitable, but it isn't permanent. When you feel like giving up, remind yourself that setbacks are not the final destination. You still have an amazing goal in front of you! It is good to take some time to process your feelings of anger and disappointment, and even reflect on what went wrong, and what you can do differently next time. But don't stay down too long. Get back to the drawing board as soon as you can and plan for your redirection.

At school: If you fail a test, exam, or grade, reassure yourself that setbacks are temporary. You have so many more opportunities to improve, as long as you believe that you can!

In sports: When you don't perform at your best in a match, don't beat yourself up about it. Look at your sports calendar and consider how many more games you have left to showcase your talent.

5. Belief: I Can Handle Whatever Comes My Way

Some challenges are scarier than others! But even the most difficult of challenges cannot put out your inner fire. Remember, there is a big "Why" motivating you to get outside of your comfort zone and do the extraordinary. That big "Why" is what keeps you putting one foot in front of the other, even when you cannot see where you are going. You are unstoppable, not because you are invincible, but because you refuse to give up!

At school: When you feel overwhelmed during a stressful school period, remind yourself about your academic goals, like receiving a scholarship to the university of your choice. Let this goal motivate you to remain focused and not derail from your day-to-day tasks.

In sports: When you are experiencing a bad season, think back to previous seasons or games where you performed really well (i.e., Received the player of the match award). Allow the positive evidence of your talent or skill to make you work harder.

Controlling Your Behaviors

Another way to resist the "I quit" mentality is to make certain behaviors, standard rules. Instead of giving yourself a choice to take action or not, make a decision that you will do it regardless of how you feel.

When David Goggins, the American ultramarathon runner, was training to lose weight, he decided that come rain or shine, he would go for his run. Even on snowy days when most people would be at home, he never missed a run. In his book, *Can't Hurt Me*, he writes "When you think that you are done, you are only 40% into what your body's capable of doing. That is just the limits that we put on ourselves".

There must always be non-negotiable behaviors that you identify, as part of achieving your goal. For Goggins, running was his non-negotiable behavior but I'm sure there were others, like consuming a specific diet. Besides behaviors, it is important to also set rules on how you speak to yourself. What are the non-negotiable words and phrases that you repeat on a daily basis, or avoid completely?

A good strategy is to avoid negative words like "can't" or "don't." These words create mental blocks, which end up becoming limiting beliefs. For example, telling yourself that you can't run a marathon rules out the possibility of ever running one. You create a mental block that prevents you from pursuing the goal or entertaining the possibility. Another example of telling yourself that you don't do something, like "I don't socialize with people." Once again, a mental block is created, and suddenly the thought of socializing becomes intimidating or undesirable.

Instead of thinking about what you can't or don't do, visualize what you can! Write a list of all the things that you can do, even if you haven't done them yet. See yourself doing what you are afraid of or believe you don't deserve. For example, if your goal is to lose weight, here is a list of all the things you CAN do:

- I can drink six to eight glasses of water a day.
- I can consume a balanced diet and cut out junk food.
- I can commit to working out for three days in a week.
- I can find a gym buddy, someone who can train with me and offer support.
- I can follow fitness experts and learn useful training tips.

Now practice saying these statements out loud. Do you notice how empowered you feel? This is the power of positive affirmation.

Continue to create your list of things that you can do below:

The "I quit" mentality can be contagious. Hang around a few people who have this type of mentality, and before you know it, you will be thinking and speaking like them too. Therefore, be careful of who you surround yourself with, the kinds of music or videos you listen to, and the content you are exposed to on social media.

Chapter Takeaways

- How you choose to see rejection and failure will determine if you can adjust to change and bounce back from the worst life circumstances. Make a choice to get rid of the "I quit" mentality and convince yourself that you have the tenacity, talent, and mindset to achieve what you want.

Since giving up is no longer an option, the next chapter of the book will show you how to apply mental toughness when dealing with difficult people.

Chapter 7: BONUS CHAPTER: Standing Your Ground When Dealing With Difficult People

If you find yourself constantly trying to prove your worth to others, you have already forgotten your value. Take a deep breath, and do what you know is right.

–Marc Chernoff

In this chapter you will learn:

- A new perspective to help you adjust how you relate to difficult people.

- How to empathize with the hardships that another person may be going through.

- Six steps to set effective boundaries, so you don't have to tolerate bad treatment in your relationships!

How to Connect with Difficult People

Engaging with difficult people is not easy. By nature, they lack empathy, which means that they may not understand the effect their behaviors have on you. For example, a difficult person might yell at you, as their way of expressing frustration, but fail to realize that by yelling, they are being disrespectful.

There are also some difficult people who believe that they are better than others, or above the law. They might demand to be treated a certain way or get easily offended when they are not given enough attention. These people are notorious for being self-centered, only showing concern or interest when they are personally affected by a situation.

Due to their lack of empathy, difficult people can emotionally trigger you to act aggressively or shut down. Naturally, you will want to put your guard up and stay far away from them. However, it isn't always possible to get away from difficult people, especially when you live with them or see them frequently at school.

The best way to manage these kinds of relationships is to proceed with understanding and adjusting how you relate to them. There are two strategies that you can adopt when relating to difficult people. The first is to do what they are unable to do, which is leading with empathy, and the second is to be assertive in how you communicate your boundaries. Let's look at both strategies together!

Developing Empathy and Understanding

It can be exhausting dealing with somebody who is comfortable receiving love and support, but barely shows love and support toward you. Or maybe when they attempt to show support, they are bad listeners and cannot create a safe space for you to express your thoughts and feelings.

But there is a healthy way to approach a difficult person, which can decrease your discomfort and frustration, and help you accept the person for who they are. This is developing an emotional intelligence skill called empathy. You have probably heard about empathy before. It is the act of putting yourself in somebody else's shoes and seeing the world from their perspective.

Showing empathy to a difficult person involves observing their behaviors without seeing them as personal attacks or creating any judgments. In other words, you acknowledge in your mind that a difficult person reacts the way they do because of what they might be going through. Their actions and behaviors are products of thoughts, beliefs, and perhaps challenging life situations that they are experiencing.

After crossing this bridge and realizing that none of what a difficult person does has to do with you, you are able to step into their shoes and imagine what pain and discomfort they might be going through.

For example, you might have a strained relationship with one of your parents because of the constant pressure they place on you to perform well at school or in a particular sport. Their behavior hurts your feelings because it makes you feel unappreciated for the hard work you put in. You might even think to yourself, "My parents don't recognize how hard I am working."

Instead of seeing their behavior as a personal attack, you can choose to show empathy. Think about the reasons why they would have such high expectations for you. For example, they may not have had access to the opportunities you have access to, and this makes them desire you to do well. Or their need to control your actions may be driven by fear of you repeating the same mistakes they did. In other words, none of what they do has anything to do with you.

The popular saying that "Hurt people, hurt people," has some truth to it. A difficult person is simply a normal person going through a difficult moment, or season in their life. This could explain why they disregard other people's feelings and only think about themselves. Out of fear, anger, guilt, grief, loneliness, or disappointment, they have learned to only think about their own well-being and security.

Therefore, you can assume that if the difficult person felt better about themselves or their life situation, they would make better choices, and be easier to be around. This type of positive assumption allows you to see the human being behind the bad behavior. Note that it doesn't excuse the bad behavior, but seeks to understand the bigger picture.

Another useful trick to help you develop empathy for a difficult person is to imagine that you have the same capacity to perform those behaviors or display that kind of attitude. If you experienced the same painful experiences as the difficult person, maybe you would feel the same way they do about life. You can also think back to the past and recall a time when you were difficult to relate with. Think about the circumstances you were going through that caused you to have a negative attitude. Can you see how being hurt can lead to hurting other people?

The more you try to understand where the difficult person is coming from, and the different factors that may be causing them to act in a particular way, you will be less offended by what they say or do. This is because you are aware that a difficult person's actions are not personal attacks. They are simply ways of expressing their own hurt feelings.

Setting your Boundaries Clearly and Effectively

The second strategy for dealing with a difficult person is to set and communicate your boundaries assertively. Boundaries are invisible limits that you create to protect yourself from being harassed or treated poorly by other people. When boundaries are communicated assertively, they are clear and direct, yet expressed with compassion.

It is important to not turn a blind eye to bad behaviors, but instead, point them out and set firm boundaries. Don't think of your boundaries as a form of punishment. They are created to protect your freedoms and teach those closest to you what kinds of behaviors are acceptable and unacceptable. You get to set the standards about the kinds of behaviors you will tolerate. If you tolerate people talking down on you, that is the standard you create. However, when and how you communicate your standards matters too. Here are a few rules to remember when preparing for the conversation about boundaries:

- Choose a convenient time for both of you to have the conversation.
- Keep the confrontation private and respectful.
- Avoid using words like "you," since it points the finger, or exaggerations like "never" or "always."
- Don't take verbal attacks personally. Remember, they reveal more about how the other person is feeling at that moment. Help them calm down by keeping your tone of voice and body language positive.

- Stick to the main topic of discussion and avoid getting sidetracked by unrelated concerns.

- Don't assume the other person knows what they did wrong. Share your thoughts and feelings as though they were unaware of their behaviors.

- Mentally and verbally rehearse what you are going to say. You may want to write notes on a piece of paper, or practice with a friend before the actual conversation. This will give you the confidence to handle the confrontation with ease!

Saying No to Unacceptable Actions and Behavior

When you have an issue with someone's behavior, such as how they are speaking or acting toward you, you can call them to the side and express your concerns. There are five steps that you can follow to set boundaries around bad behavior, which include:

1. Own Your Problem

Clearly state that you have a problem and explain what it is. Use an "I" statement to show ownership of your experience. Take this opportunity to also check whether it is a good time to discuss your concern. If not, arrange a more suitable time. For example, if you would like to raise a concern with one of your teachers about the way they spoke to you in class, you could say something like this:

"Miss Tracy, I have a problem with the manner in which you spoke to me in class today. When is it a good time for us to have a chat?"

2. Explain the Value Violation

The reason why the behavior was offensive is that it violated one of your core values. Describe to the other person which values were violated. For example, if one of your friends has sworn at you, and has made you feel disrespected, you can say:

"Tommy, mutual respect is something that I value in friendships because it shows me that you accept me for who I am. This is why I felt so offended when you swore at me."

3. Describe the Bad Behavior and Emotional Impact

Next, describe how the other person behaved, assuming that they don't have a clue about how they may have offended you. Afterward, mention how their behavior made you feel. For example, if you had a disagreement with your coach, and they made you feel small, you can say:

"Coach Felix, while I was talking, you yelled at me and told me to keep quiet. I felt angry and unappreciated."

4. Suggest an Alternative Behavior

Share with the other person what you would like to see happen. In other words, explain the appropriate behavior that they can display next time. For example, if one of your friends has a tendency of teasing you in front of other people, you can suggest an alternative behavior, such as:

"Kate, moving forward, I will not tolerate being spoken down to. When we are having conversations between us or amongst other

people, please be considerate of your choice of words. I won't accept name calling anymore, even if it is a joke."

5. Enforce Consequences

To make sure that the other person knows how serious you are about maintaining your boundaries, enforce consequences for future boundary violations. Explain to them what will happen if they mistakenly commit the same bad behavior again.

When thinking about consequences, find an action that will reinforce the core value you want to be protected. For example, if you value punctuality, you can leave when your friend arrives more than 30 minutes late to a lunch date. When setting consequences, use the "If... then..." statement. For example:

"If you cuss at me again, then I will disengage from the conversation and walk away immediately (this reinforces your need for mutual respect)."

Now it is your turn! Think about a recent situation where a friend or family behaved poorly toward you. Choose a behavior that violates one of your core values. Follow the five steps outlined above to set clear boundaries.

1. **Own Your Problem**

2. **Explain the Value Violation**

3. Describe the Bad Behavior and Emotional Impact

4. Suggest an Alternative Behavior

5. Enforce Consequences

Chapter Takeaways

- Difficult people have a way of getting under our skin and bringing out the worst side of our personalities. However, how difficult people behave should never be treated as personal attacks. Their behaviors should be seen as clues to how they are feeling about themselves, and the painful situations they may be going through.

- When dealing with a difficult person, lead with empathy. Put yourself in their shoes and imagine the factors that may be causing the negative attitude. Try to imagine how similarly you would behave if you were dealing with similar issues.

As compassionate as you should be toward a difficult person, it is never okay to excuse bad behavior. You deserve to be treated with the same respect you show to others. Have the courage to speak up for yourself and set clear boundaries. Be direct about what you will no longer tolerate, and the consequences for crossing your boundary in the future.

Conclusion

Increasing the state of our minds is the only way to reduce the difficulty of life.

–Mokokoma Mokhonoana

It takes a lot of courage to expose yourself to the situations you fear the most. But when this happens, you can learn a lot about yourself, such as your hidden talents, strengths, and weaknesses, as well as the type of lifestyle you desire to create. Therefore, there is value in charging directly into the storms of your life because when you eventually get out of those challenging situations, you come out stronger and more focused than you have ever been!

Throughout this handbook, you have learned how to apply mental toughness in everyday life situations, so you can maintain a positive and flexible outlook on your life, despite the challenges you encounter. Feel free to refer to the handbook, or specific exercises inside, whenever you need a reminder of how to regain control of your thoughts, emotions, and behaviors.

Your journey to becoming mentally tough has already begun. Enjoy the process of becoming the more resilient version of yourself!

Thank You

Dear reader, I would like to take this time to appreciate you. Without your purchase and interest, I wouldn't be able to keep writing helpful books like this one. Once again, THANK YOU for reading this book. I hope you enjoyed it as much as I enjoyed writing it.

Before you go, I have a small favor to ask of you. **Would you please consider posting a review of this book on the platform? Posting a review will help support my writing.**

Your feedback is very important and will help me continue to provide more informative literature in the future. I look forward to hearing from you.

Just use the relevant link below.

USA - https://amazon.com/review/create-review/?&asin=B0BTJ4JB8W

UK - https://amazon.co.uk/review/create-review/?&asin=B0BTJ4JB8W

Canada - https://amazon.ca/review/create-review/?&asin=B0BTJ4JB8W

References

Abika. (n.d.). Zen stories to tell your neighbours. In Arvind Gupta Toys. https://www.arvindguptatoys.com/arvindgupta/zen-for-neighbours.pdf

Bathla, S. (2019, May 20). 6 Types of thinking patterns and what should be yours? Medium. https://medium.com/@sombathla/6-types-of-thinking-patterns-and-what-should-be-yours-acc498492b5a

Bolland, P. (2016, June 23). Thinking through: The rock of sisyphus. Peter Bolland. http://peterbolland.blogspot.com/2016/06/the-rock-of-sisyphus.html

Branch, R., & Willson, R. (2012). Cognitive behavioural therapy workbook for dummies, 2nd ed. John Wiley & Sons.

Brian, P. (2021, September 26). 25 Resilient people who overcame failure to achieve huge success. Ideapod.com. https://ideapod.com/resilient-people-who-overcame-failure-to-achieve-huge-success/

Chernoff, M. (2016, June 5). 12 Quotes that will bring peace when you deal with difficult people. Marc and Angel Hack Life. https://www.marcandangel.com/2016/06/05/12-quotes-that-will-bring-peace-when-you-deal-with-difficult-people/

Cherry, K. (2022, October 17). How resilience helps with the coping of crisis. Verywell Mind. https://www.verywellmind.com/what-is-resilience-2795059

Cooks-Campbell, A. (2022, April 11). What do you want in life? 11 Questions and tips to figure it out. Www.betterup.com. https://www.betterup.com/blog/what-do-i-want

Doorn, M. van. (2019, June 17). You are the average of the five people you spend the most time with. Medium. https://maartenvandoorn.medium.com/you-are-the-average-of-the-five-people-you-spend-the-most-time-with-a2ea32d08c72#:~:text=In%20the%20words%20of%20motivational

Duhigg, C. (2011). How habits work. Charles Duhigg. https://charlesduhigg.com/how-habits-work/

Duhigg, C. (2014). Power of habit : Why we do what we do in life and business. Random House Trade Paperbacks.

Dweck, C. S. (2006). Mindset : The new psychology of success. Ballantine Books.

Embogama. (2016, August 5). Difference between conscious and subconscious mind. Definition, comparison of functions and processes. Pediaa.com. https://pediaa.com/difference-between-conscious-and-subconscious-mind/

Eurosport. (2016, March 19). Cristiano Ronaldo: Hard work is vital to my success. Eurosport; Eurosport. https://www.eurosport.com/football/cristiano-ronaldo-hard-work-is-vital-to-my-success_sto5324288/story.shtml

Fabrega, M. (2016, March 9). How to not give up – 8 Strategies for not quitting. Daringtolivefully.com. https://daringtolivefully.com/how-to-not-give-up

Goleman, D. (n.d.). 4 Emotional intelligence skills for handling crises. Www.kornferry.com. https://www.kornferry.com/insights/this-week-in-leadership/emotional-intelligence-skills-coronavirus-leadership#:~:text=The%20four%20domains%20of%20Emotional

Goleman, D. (2005). Emotional intelligence. Bantam Books.

> Good Reads. (n.d.-a). *David Goggins quotes (author of Can't Hurt Me)*. Www.goodreads.com.

https://www.goodreads.com/author/quotes/17977069.David_Goggins

Good Reads. (n.d.-a). Germany Kent quote. Www.goodreads.com. https://www.goodreads.com/author/show/8557658.Germany_Kent

Good Reads. (n.d.-b). Sadie Robertson quote. Www.goodreads.com. https://www.goodreads.com/author/show/8209245.Sadie_Robertson

Good Reads. (n.d.-c). The power of your subconscious mind quotes by Joseph Murphy. Www.goodreads.com. https://www.goodreads.com/work/quotes/2037992-putting-the-power-of-your-subconscious-mind-to-work#:~:text=%E2%80%9CJust%20keep%20your%20conscious%20mind

Griffin, T. (2022, September 1). Learning from failure: Valuable lessons to remember. Business.com. https://www.business.com/articles/learning-from-failure/

Hurley, K. (2022, July 14). What is resilience? Definition, types, building resiliency, benefits and resources | everyday health. EverydayHealth.com. https://www.everydayhealth.com/wellness/resilience/

Indeed Editorial Team. (2021, June 4). 8 Tips for how to work hard. Indeed Career Guide. https://www.indeed.com/career-advice/career-development/tips-for-how-to-work-hard

Indeed Editorial Team. (2022, September 16). What does it mean to work hard? Indeed Career Guide. https://ca.indeed.com/career-advice/career-development/work-hard#:~:text=Hard%20work%20is%20going%20above

Jewell, T., & Hoshaw, C. (2021, November 5). Diaphragmatic breathing: Exercises, techniques, and more. Healthline. https://www.healthline.com/health/diaphragmatic-breathing#steps

Kelly, D. C. (2022, September 27). 48 Quotes about hard work that'll help you reach your goals. Blog.hubspot.com. https://blog.hubspot.com/sales/hard-work-quotes

Kihu, M. (2019, April 1). 5 Ways to hack your subconscious mind and unlock your greatest life. Fearless Soul. https://iamfearlesssoul.com/hack-your-subconscious-mind/

Killoren, C. (2021, January 13). 52 Romantic questions for getting to know your partner better. Hellorelish.com. https://hellorelish.com/articles/romantic-questions-to-ask-your-partner.html

Lagudu, S. (2022, September 19). 51 Inspirational quotes about teenagers life. MomJunction. https://www.momjunction.com/articles/teen-life-quotes_00462262/

Laurinavicius, T. (2022, October 12). 30 Badass mental toughness quotes to inspire you to push harder. Best Writing. https://bestwriting.com/quotes/mental-toughness

Leaf, C. (2021, March 8). How are the mind and the brain different? A neuroscientist explains. Mindbodygreen. https://www.mindbodygreen.com/articles/difference-between-mind-and-brain-neuroscientist

Mavi, M. (2018, May 15). 10 Things highly disciplined people have in common. Atrium. https://www.atriumstaff.com/10-things-highly-disciplined-people-have-in-common/

Mayberry, M. (2017, January 18). 10 Great quotes on the power of goals. Entrepreneur.

https://www.entrepreneur.com/leadership/10-great-quotes-on-the-power-of-goals/287411

Melman, C. (2012, October 17). 5 Things that Cristiano Ronaldo does better than Lionel Messi. Bleacher Report. https://bleacherreport.com/articles/1373932-5-things-that-cristiano-ronaldo-does-better-than-lionel-messi

Mental Toughness Partners. (2016, October 26). Key signs that you're mentally stronger than most. Www.mentaltoughness.partners. https://www.mentaltoughness.partners/mentally-stronger/

Mental Toughness Partners. (2022). What is mental toughness? Www.mentaltoughness.partners. https://www.mentaltoughness.partners/what-is-mental-toughness/

Morgan, P. (n.d.). Easy scripts for hard conversations. Solutions for Resilience. https://www.solutionsforresilience.com/hard-conversations/

Mr. Curry. (2016, March 26). "Discipline is choosing between what you want now and what you want most." — Abraham Lincoln – Lee's Martial Arts. Leesbloomington. https://www.leesbloomington.com/2016/03/26/discipline-is-choosing-between-what-you-want-now-and-what-you-want-most-abraham-lincoln/

Nair, K. (2021, September 22). Cristiano Ronaldo defies age, clocks 32.51 km/h to become fastest player on field. Republic World. https://www.republicworld.com/sports-news/cricket-news/cristiano-ronaldo-defies-age-clocks-32-dot-51-km-h-to-become-fastest-player-on-field.html

Olusola, L. (2020, August 20). Emotional mastery: Why it matters! The Guardian Nigeria News.

https://guardian.ng/features/emotional-mastery-why-it-matters/

Outreach. (2021, November 19). Negative thought patterns and depression. Sage Neuroscience Center. https://sageclinic.org/blog/negative-thoughts-depression/

Owaves. (2021, January 15). Day in the life: Cristiano Ronaldo, soccer legend. Owaves.com. https://owaves.com/day-plan/day-life-cristiano-ronaldo/

Pallas, A. (2021, July 7). 5 Strategies to develop empathy for "difficult" people. Www.linkedin.com. https://www.linkedin.com/pulse/5-strategies-develop-empathy-difficult-people-alexandra-pallas/

Peer, M. (2019, June 6). The differences between your conscious and subconscious mind. Marisa Peer. https://marisapeer.com/the-differences-between-your-conscious-and-subconscious-mind/

Potts, N. (2020, December 9). "Discipline is choosing between what you want now and what you want most." Abraham Lincoln. Www.linkedin.com. https://www.linkedin.com/pulse/discipline-choosing-between-what-you-want-now-most-abraham-potts/

Ribeiro, M. (2019, April 9). How to be mentally strong: 14 Ways to build mental toughness. PositivePsychology.com. https://positivepsychology.com/mentally-strong/#improve

Ringer, J. (2019). We have to talk: A step-by-step checklist for difficult conversations. Judy Ringer. https://www.judyringer.com/resources/articles/we-have-to-talk-a-stepbystep-checklist-for-difficult-conversations.php

Romano, C. (2014, May 26). 10 Ways to identify your talents and utilize them. Lifehack.

https://www.lifehack.org/articles/productivity/10-ways-identify-your-talents-and-utilize-them.html

Russell, T. (2021, June 27). Why habit loop theory might change your life in small ways. Greatist. https://greatist.com/happiness/habit-loop#breaking-habits

Tardi, C. (2022, July 7). How to apply the 80-20 rule. Investopedia. https://www.investopedia.com/terms/1/80-20-rule.asp

Torres, E. (2021, October 4). 99 Positive affirmations you can use daily. The Good Trade. https://www.thegoodtrade.com/features/positive-affirmations-morning-routine

Traugott, J. (2014, August 26). Achieving your goals: An evidence-based approach. MSU Extension. https://www.canr.msu.edu/news/achieving_your_goals_an_evidence_based_approach

Vaughn, K. (2018, June 10). 5 Things to say to yourself when you want to quit. Medium. https://kassandravaughn.medium.com/5-things-to-say-to-yourself-when-you-want-to-quit-b9e9be73ea54

Whitaker, A. (2020, May 4). What are your natural talents and abilities? (article 4). Www.linkedin.com. https://www.linkedin.com/pulse/what-your-natural-talents-abilities-article-4-anne-whitaker/

Wilczek, F. (2015, Sept 23). Einstein's parable of quantum insanity. Scientific American. https://www.scientificamerican.com/article/einstein-s-parable-of-quantum-insanity/#:~:text=%E2%80%9CInsanity%20is%20doing%20the%20same

www.ingramcontent.com/pod-product-compliance
Lightning Source LLC
Chambersburg PA
CBHW030309100526
44590CB00012B/573